This special edition of
The Dhammapada
is published to commemorate
the 100th birthday of

·

Venerable Ananda Maitreya

·

August 23, 1995

The Dhammapada

The Path of Truth

TRANSLATED BY
**The Venerable
Balangoda Ananda Maitreya**

REVISED BY
Rose Kramer

PARALLAX PRESS

Parallax Press
P.O. Box 7355
Berkeley, California 94707

For all of their help and inspiration, thanks to Ken McLeod,
Gregory Kramer, Marcy Weinberg, and the Most Venerable
Kalu Rinpoche.

Front cover photo illustration based on a photograph
by Don Farber
Back cover photo by Don Farber
Cover design by Legacy Media, Inc.
Text design by Abigail Johnston

Library of Congress Cataloging-in-Publication Data
    Tipitaka. Suttapitaka. Khuddakanikaya. Dhammapada.
    English.
        The Dhammapada: the path of truth/translated by
    Balangoda Ananda Maitreya; revised by Rose Kramer. I.
    Anandamaitreya, Balangoda, Nayaka Sthavira. II. Kramer,
    Rose. III. Title.
    BQ1372.E54A53 1995
    294.3'823—dc19   88-13060
    ISBN 0-938077-87-2

Contents

		Preface	vii
		Publisher's Preface	xiii
1	·	Twins	1
2	·	Mindfulness	5
3	·	Mind	9
4	·	Flowers	13
5	·	The Fool	17
6	·	The Wise	21
7	·	The Arahant	25
8	·	Thousands	29
9	·	Evil	33
10	·	The Rod	37
11	·	Old Age	41
12	·	Self	45
13	·	The World	47
14	·	The Buddha	51

15	·	Happiness	55
16	·	The Pleasant	59
17	·	Anger	63
18	·	Blemishes	67
19	·	The Righteous	71
20	·	The Way	75
21	·	Miscellany	79
22	·	State of Woe	83
23	·	The Elephant	87
24	·	Craving	91
25	·	The Bhikkhu	97
26	·	Noble One	103

Preface

The Dhammapada holds a special place of distinction in Buddhist literature. It is often characterized as the most representative example of the teachings of the Buddha. It provides, beautifully and simply, a key to the fundamentals of early Buddhist philosophy and has been translated from the original Pali into more languages than any other Buddhist text, including English, French, German, Danish, Chinese, and Hindi.

The message of the Dhammapada is relevant to our time, a poetic and philosophical bridge between East and West at a time when oceans no longer provide the vast separations of the past. It points to a way of life and attitudes that emphasize harmony and oneness with all living beings. Its message of right action is timeless as well as timely, reflecting the spirit of Buddha's teaching method, and speaks to the perfectability of humankind and to the scientific impeccability of the law of cause and effect. The Dhammapada does not indulge in intellectual speculation. Life is enhanced and ultimately perfected by inward development. To the seeker there is provided a grounded moral philosophy, with no references to a savior.

In his *Wisdom of China and India,* the philosopher Lin Yutang calls the Dhammapada "a great spiritual testimony, one of the very few religious masterpieces of the world, combining genuineness of spiritual passion with a happy gift of literary expression."

This version of the Dhammapada has been derived from the translation by one of the most highly regarded teachers in the Theravada Buddhist world today. He is the ninety-four-year-old scholar and Buddhist missionary, The Most Venerable Aggamahapandita Balangoda Ananda Maitreya Mahanayaka Thera. The Ven. Ananda Maitreya became a monk in 1911 in Sri Lanka, and at an early age gained the reputation as an outstanding teacher. He is known throughout the scholarly community as both a master in the Theravada and Mahayana schools of Buddhism, as well as of Pali, Sanskrit, and several other languages. He served as chairman of the Department of Buddhist Philosophy and as Dean of the Faculty of Oriental Studies at the University of Sri Lanka, Vidyodaya Campus. He was the Vice-

Chancellor of the same university campus at the time of his retirement in 1965.

The Ven. Maitreya served for many years as the Supreme Chief of the Amarapura sect, and as advisor and translator of the Tripitaka Translation Committee after his appointment by the government of Sri Lanka. He was the chairman of the monks who actively participated in the famous Sixth Council held in Burma in 1953. Since his retirement he has been lecturing in the United States, United Kingdom, Canada, Australia, and wherever his unique and extensive experience and abilities are needed.

Along with his ongoing regimen of research, translating, writing, and teaching classes all over the world, the Ven. Maitreya is a well-known meditation teacher of vast experience and background. As a young man he practiced Hindu Yoga under Indian teachers in addition to Buddhist meditation techniques. He now teaches both samatha (calm meditation) and vipassana (insight meditation). His appearance on the program "Footprints of the Buddha," a segment of the BBC series "The Long Search," has been widely viewed both in the United Kingdom and on public television in the United States.

Rose Kramer is a general semanticist, special educator, seminar leader, Phi Beta Kappa, and Bachelor of Arts from New York University

(Washington Square College), and received her Master of Science degree as a Graduate Fellow at the University of Southern California. She holds a California Life Credential in the Humanities and practices vipassana (insight meditation). Ms. Kramer is President of the Foundation for Human Development. Her most recent lectures include those on "The Art of Living," "Creative Aging," and "Self-Esteem."

When Ms. Kramer submitted this version of the Dhammapada to the publishers she wrote: "The road to my involvement with the Dhammapada has been a gradual and organic one. Life experiences, formal education, psychotherapy, sensitivity training, and encounter groups led me to the 'vacant lot' on which I was to build my new house of consciousness at age forty. An important discovery was meditation practice. I found the Buddhist practice of vipassana most natural for me, and have been enriched and advanced by teachers and guides over the years. It has been my good fortune to have meditated under the guidance of Anagarika Dhammadina, Jack Kornfeld, Joseph Goldstein, Stephen Levine, and the Ven. Ananda Maitreya, as well as other excellent teachers.

"When I first met the Ven. Ananda Maitreya, I felt not the weight but the lightness of his then ninety-one years. He gave me a small red volume of eighty-two pages which I leafed through. It was his translation of the Dhammapada. Opening to a page at random I asked, 'What is a "fletcher"?' When he responded 'An arrowsmith,' I pointed out that most Westerners would not recognize this term. At that moment he invited me to undertake the task that I have embraced with joy for the last three years. This has been to render his translation more accessible to a wider and specifically Western readership by updating the language to current usage. In the process the Dhammapada has become a beacon of wisdom, humor, and poetry for me."

METTA FOUNDATION

Publisher's Preface

A number of versions of the Dhammapada, the revered Pali compilation of the Buddha's essential teachings, are available in English today. While all these editions have merit, a definitive translation has yet to be published. Therefore, it is with great pleasure that we make this version of the Dhammapada available, for it is the first truly authoritative edition to appear in English.

Translated from the Pali by the Venerable Ananda Maitreya, a highly respected Theravada monk and an accomplished scholar of Buddhism, the text was revised by Rose Kramer, a noted American semanticist and educator. Her revisions were fastidiously rechecked by the Ven. Ananda Maitreya to ensure the authenticity of the translation. The result of such painstaking effort is a translation of the Dhammapada that is at once impeccably accurate and highly accessible to modern Western readers.

The Dhammapada was originally compiled for the growing community of Buddhist monks; it served as a basic guide for following the Buddha's teachings. Because its audience was primarily male, the language may sound a bit one-sided to modern readers. We have chosen, however, to remain true to the original text for in the end it is the teachings themselves that are important. Regardless of the limitations of language and culture, the wisdom of the Buddha transcends time and space and directly speaks to the heart of all humanity.

We are honored to present this edition of the Dhammapada—we hope that in its pages you will find inspiration and guidance. The Ven. Ananda Maitreya has said: "If I were to recommend one book of all the Buddhist scriptures, it would be the Dhammapada. It contains all the wisdom of the Buddha; it is all you need."

1

Twins

1 Mind is the forerunner of all actions.
All deeds are led by mind, created by mind.
If one speaks or acts with a corrupt mind,
    suffering follows,
As the wheel follows the hoof of an ox pulling
    a cart.

2 Mind is the forerunner of all actions.
All deeds are led by mind, created by mind.
If one speaks or acts with a serene mind,
    happiness follows,
As surely as one's shadow.

3 "He abused me, mistreated me, defeated me,
    robbed me."
Harboring such thoughts keeps hatred alive.

4 "He abused me, mistreated me, defeated me,
    robbed me."
Releasing such thoughts banishes hatred for all
    time.

5 Animosity does not eradicate animosity.
  Only by loving kindness is animosity dissolved.
  This law is ancient and eternal.

6 There are those who are aware
  That we are always facing death.
  Knowing this, they put aside all contentiousness.

7 The one who lives for sensation,
  Unrestrained, indulgent in eating, irreverent,
     lazy,
  The tempter Mara* breaks,
  Just as the wind breaks a frail tree.

8 The one who lives mindfully, senses under
     control,
  Moderate in eating, devout, energetic,
  Cannot be overthrown by Mara,
  Just as the wind cannot shake a rocky mountain.

9 The monk's robe does not in itself
  Render one free from stain.
  If the one who wears that robe
  Is lacking in self-control and honesty,
  He is unworthy of such a robe.

10 Only one who is free from stain,
   Well-disciplined, honest,

*Mara: In Buddhist scriptures Mara is a metaphor for temptations
or passions personified, being neither male nor female; hence,
the use of "tempter."

And endowed with self-control,
Is worthy of the monk's robe.

11 Those who fail to distinguish
The nonessential from the essential
And the essential from the nonessential,
Will, in feeding on wrong thoughts,
Fail to attain the essential.

12 On the other hand, those who correctly perceive
The essential as essential
And the nonessential as nonessential
Will, in feeding on right thoughts,
Attain the essential.

13 As rain pours through badly thatched houses,
So does desire penetrate the undeveloped mind.

14 As rain fails to pour through a well-thatched
house,
So does desire fail to penetrate the
well-developed mind.

15 For the doer of evil there is only grief,
Here as well as hereafter.
In both states he experiences grief,
Seeing his own unwholesome acts.

16 For the doer of good deeds there is rejoicing,
Here as well as hereafter.
Joy and more joy are his,
As he sees his own right action.

17 The doer of evil reaps suffering,
Here and hereafter,
In both states remembering, "I have
committed evil."
Not only here, but hereafter, he experiences
more suffering,
Because he has gone to a state of suffering.

18 The doer of good deeds reaps happiness,
Here and hereafter,
In both states remembering, "I have done
good deeds."
And there is more joy,
Because he has gone to a blissful state.

19 A careless person,
Quoting much of the scriptural text
but not living it,
Cannot share the abundance of the holy life,
Just as the cowherd, counting other people's
cattle,
Cannot taste the milk or ghee.

20 Reciting a small portion of the scriptures,
But putting it diligently into practice;
Letting go of passion, aggression, and
confusion;
Revering the truth with a clear mind;
And not clinging to anything,
here or hereafter;
Brings the harvest of the holy life.

2

Mindfulness

1 Mindfulness is the path to immortality.
   Negligence is the path to death.
   The vigilant never die,
   Whereas the negligent are the living dead.

2 With this understanding,
   The wise, having developed a high degree of
       mindfulness,
   Rejoice in mindfulness,
   Paying heed to each step on the path.

3 These awakened ones,
   Dedicated to meditation,
   Striving actively and vigorously,
   Attain nirvana, the ultimate security.

4 The radiance of the man who is committed,
   Aware, unsullied,
   Acting with consideration and restraint,
   Becomes more luminous.

5 The wise man,
By vigor, mindfulness, restraint, and
self-control,
Creates for himself an island
Which no flood can submerge.

6 The foolish, the unwise,
Surrender themselves to negligence,
Whereas the wise man protects mindfulness
As his most valuable possession.

7 "Don't lose yourself in negligence,
Don't lose yourself in sensuality."
These admonitions lead to joy and fulfillment
In the mindful and meditative man.

8 When the enlightened man frees himself
From careless behavior through mindfulness,
Free of sorrow, he gazes on the sorrowing
masses,
As one on the mountaintop gazes on the plain
below.

9 The mindful person among the mindless,
The aware person among the unaware,
Surpasses the rest with his wisdom,
Like a superb racehorse outstripping an old
worn-out horse.

10 By mindfulness did the Maghavat,* Lord of
    Two Realms,
    Reach a position of authority among the gods.
    So does mindfulness ever surpass carelessness.

11 A seeker,** concentrating on mindfulness,
    Advances like a fire,
    Consuming the chains of bondage
    Both great and small.

12 A monk, or lay person, rejoicing in mindfulness,
    Seeing the danger of negligence,
    Is protected on the way to his perfect state
    And is close to nirvana.

*Maghavat: According to the belief of ancient Indians, Maghavat
was the king of a certain heavenly realm. He was born into that
realm and became its overlord as a result of good deeds he had
performed in his immediate previous life as a man on earth. During
that time he fulfilled all his duties toward others mindfully.

*Seeker: Originally the term here was bhikkhu, or monk. When
the Buddha was speaking to his hearers the bhikkhus were
always sitting near him. That is why in his general talks he
addressed monks. One meaning of bhikku is "One who
discerns the fears of the round of rebirths."

3

Mind

1 Just as an arrowsmith shapes an arrow to
        perfection with fire,
    So does the wise man shape his mind,
    Which is fickle, unsteady, vulnerable, and
        erratic.

2 Like a fish taken from the safety of its watery
        home
    And cast upon the dry land,
    So does this mind flutter, due to the lure of the
        tempter.
    Therefore one should leave the dominion of
        Mara.

3 How good it is to rein the mind,
    Which is unruly, capricious, rushing wherever
        it pleases.
    The mind so harnessed will bring one happiness.

4 A wise man should pay attention to his mind,
   Which is very difficult to perceive.
   It is extremely subtle and wanders wherever it
       pleases.
   The mind, well-guarded and controlled,
   Will bring him happiness.

5 One who keeps a rein on the wandering mind,
   Which strays far and wide, alone, bodiless,
   Will be freed from the tyranny of the tempter.

6 A man of fickle mind
   Will never attain wisdom to its fullest,
   Since he is ignorant of the Dhamma
   And has wavering faith.

7 The heart of the fully conscious man
       is fearless—
   He has freed his mind of lust and anger,
   He has transcended both good and evil.

8 Observe this body, as fragile as an earthen vase.
   Build a mind as solid as a fortified city,
   Then confront Mara with the weapon of
       insight
   And (proceeding without attachment)
   Guard what you have already conquered.

9 Certainly before long this body will lie on the
       ground,

Lifeless and unconscious,
Cast aside like a useless log.

10 A mind out of control will do more harm
Than two angry men engaged in combat.

11 A well-directed mind creates more well-being
Than the wholesome actions of parents
Toward their children.

4

Flowers

1 Who can truly see this earth, this body,
  This world of human beings, as well as the
    realm of gods?
  Who is able to distill the wisdom of the
    Dhamma
  As skillfully as a designer of garlands
    selects choice flowers?

2 Sekha,* a trainee on the first stage of
    perfection,
  Is able to grasp this earth, the human world,
  The dwellings of the unhappy ones,
  As well as the realm of the gods.

Sekha: Literally means "a trainee," but it also refers to the person who entered the state of the streamwinners level, where he experiences for the first time the full vision of nirvana. From that stage onwards, until he attains *arahantship* (perfection), he is called *sekha,* one who is still on the path to perfection.

He can bring forth the shining truth of the
   Dhamma,
Even as a skillful gardener selects choice
   flowers.

3 See this body, as fragile and transient as foam.
Know that it is as insubstantial as a mirage,
And thereby avoid the lure of the tempter's
   flowery arrows,
And put yourself beyond death's grasp.

4 Just as a raging flood sweeps away a sleeping
   village,
So does death claim a man of distracted mind,
As he continually seeks more and more
Of life's fleeting pleasures.

5 Death drowns the unsatisfied man,
Whose restless mind clutches
For greater and greater pleasures.

6 The wise man goes gently through the village,
Like a bee extracting honey from the flower
But leaving the color and fragrance intact.

7 Pay no attention to harsh words uttered by
   others.
Do not be concerned with what others have
   or have not done.
Observe your own actions and inactions.

8 Like a beautiful brightly colored flower without
       fragrance
    Is the well-spoken word without action.

9 Like a beautiful brightly colored flower full of
       fragrance
    Is the well-spoken word and the deed that
       matches the word.

10 A man born to this world should do many
       good deeds,
    As a garland maker makes garlands from
       a heap of flowers.

11 The scent of flowers is carried
    No farther than the wind allows,
    Neither the sandalwood, tagar, nor jasmine.
    But the fragrance of the deeds of good men
       spreads
    To the ends of the earth, in all directions,
    Regardless of the wind.

12 The aroma of sandalwood, tagar,
    Lotus, or vassiki is excellent.
    Superior to these is the fragrance of right action,
    Right speech, and right way of earning one's
       living.

13 The scent of tagar and sandalwood may be
       barely detectable,

Whereas the fragrance of the virtuous
Reaches the highest levels,
Both among gods and men.

14 Mara, the tempter, can never find
Where the enlightened ones are,
For they live mindfully and in perfect freedom
Through perfect knowledge.

15, Just as a sweet-smelling lotus blooms
16 Beside the highway upon a heap of filth,
So does the disciple of the perfect Buddha
Rise above those bound blindly
To the limitations of the world.

5

The Fool

1 Long is the night to the sleepless.
Long is the road to the weary traveler.
Long is the cycle of rebirths to the unwise,
Who do not know the truth.

2 Should a traveler fail to find a companion
Equal or better,
Rather than suffer the company of a fool,
He should resolutely walk alone.

3 "I have children; I have wealth."
These are the empty claims of an unwise man.
If he cannot call himself his own,
How can he then claim children and wealth as
his own?

4 To the extent that a fool knows his foolishness,
He may be deemed wise.
A fool who considers himself wise
Is indeed a fool.

5 A fool may associate with a wise man throughout
      his life
   And remain untouched by his wisdom,
   Even as a spoon cannot taste the flavor of soup.

6 On the other hand, an aware man, in a moment's
      meeting,
   Can learn from a wise man,
   Even as the tongue tastes the flavor of soup.

7 The unwise man, lacking understanding,
   Behaves as if he were his own worst enemy,
   Committing evil deeds
   That produce bitter fruit.

8 It is unwise to do things that bring regret
   And require repentance,
   To cause suffering for oneself
   And a weeping and tearful face.

9 It is wise to do things which do not require
      repentance
   But bring joy and fulfillment,
   Happiness and delight.

10 Until he feels the effect,
   The fool rejoices in his evil deed
   When the action reaches fruition,
   The fool harvests nothing but grief.

11 Though the fool may practice asceticism,
   Eating a speck of food on the tip of a blade
      of grass,

He is not worth one-sixteenth of the arahant,
The knower of the Dhamma.

12 An evil deed does not produce its results
        at once.*
   It smolders slowly, like a fire covered by ashes,
   And finally consumes its doer, the fool.

13 The things a fool gains amount to nothing.
   Unwholesome acts cannot bring him wholesome
        results.

14, What a fool hungers for
15 Is false fame, authority,
   Power over others, and generous offerings.
   He seeks recognition as a doer,
   A wielder of power,
   A knower of right and wrong.
   His craving and pride are insatiable.

16 There is a path that leads to worldly gain.
   Another road leads to nirvana.
   Let the seeker, the disciple of Buddha,
   Embracing seclusion,
   Take the path to wisdom and enlightenment.

*In the original text, this verse reads: "An evil deed, like milk
freshly drawn from the udder,/Does not produce its results at
once." When the Dhammapada was compiled this metaphor
would have been relevant to those familiar with the problem
of keeping milk fresh in a hot climate without the aid of
refrigeration. To the modern reader this metaphor of spoiled
milk may appear confusing; thus, we have omitted it for the
sake of clarity and ease in reading the text.

6

The Wise

1 If someone sees an intelligent person
Who is skillfully able to point out shortcomings,
And give suitable reproof,
Let him cherish such a revealer of hidden
    treasures.
Only good can come from such an association.

2 Let the wise one guide, correct,
And deter others from what is base and vile.
He will be treasured by the good and spurned
    by the evil.

3 Do not choose bad friends.
Do not choose persons of low habits.
Select good friends. Be discriminating.
Choose the best.

4 Whoever drinks deeply of Dhamma lives
    happily,
With a peaceful mind.

The wise man rejoices in the Dhamma
Taught by the holy ones.

5 Irrigators contain the flowing waters.
Arrowsmiths fashion arrows.
Carpenters shape wood to their design.
Wise men mold their characters.

6 As a solid rock stands firm in the wind,
Even so is a wise man unmoved by praise or
blame.

7 As a deep lake remains still and clear,
So do wise men, listening to the teachings,
Attain a serene mind.

8 The good certainly cling to nothing.
They do not talk aimlessly, concerned with
personal gains.
The wise, the saintly,
Whether experiencing comfort or discomfort,
Show neither elation nor depression.

9 Not for one's own or another's gain
Should one commit an evil deed.
Regardless of the desire for children, wealth,
or kingdom,
Or any other kind of success,
One should remain virtuous, wise, and
righteous.

10 The few cross over to the far shore.
   The many merely run back and forth fruitlessly
   Along the side of the stream.

11 But only those who follow the carefully taught
       law
   Can cross to the other shore,
   Beyond the grasp of death, so hard to overcome.

12, Let the wise man shun the cauldron
13   of confusion,
   And proceed on the path of light.
   Let him leave the comfort of home,
   Forsaking sensual pleasures,
   Freeing himself from all obstacles,
   Delighting in seclusion
   (Not an ordinary man's choice),
   And devote himself to cleansing the
       blemishes of the mind.

14 Those who have carefully cultivated
       their minds
   In tune with the elements of enlightenment—
   Who, without grasping, delight in
       detachment,
   Cleansed of all corruption and therefore
       shining brightly,
   Send forth brilliant light.

7

The Arahant

1 There is no burning for him who has completed
   the journey,
   Who is free of sorrows and all else,
   And who has broken off all chains.

2 The mindful put forth great effort.
   They do not remain content in the household
   life
   But leave their homes behind,
   Just as swans leave a muddy lake.

3 The mind that clings to nothing
   And takes a right view of eating,
   Focused on deliverance,
   Leaves no trace, like the path of birds in the
   sky.
   Such a mind is free from desire and the like.

4 He who is free from obsessions—
   Eating simply, clear-headed, and focused on
       liberation—
   Like a migrating bird,
   Leaves no trace of a track in the sky.

5 Even the gods delight in the presence of one
   Who has freed himself from pride and
       mental obsessions,
   Who has his senses under control,
   Like horses trained by an expert trainer.

6 Done with the round of rebirths,
   He is as accepting as the earth,
   As firm as a doorpost,
   Placid as a pond free of mud, and dutiful.

7 Whoever has reached a state of freedom
   Through perfect wisdom,
   Peaceful and unshakable,
   Is nonviolent in his mind, his speech, his
       action.

8 Whoever is in touch with the infinite,
   Free of attachment,
   Desireless,
   Is the highest among men.

9 Delightful is the place where the saints dwell,
   Be it village or forest,
   Cavern or open field.

10 Delightful are forests, where more worldly
        men find no joy,
    Being free of the pull of desire.
    Saints, who seek no worldly pleasures,
    Find delight in such places.

8

Thousands

1 A single wise word bringing peace to the
      listener
   Is worth more than a thousand speeches
   Full of empty words.

2 A single verse full of meaning
   Bringing peace to the listener
   Is worth more than a thousand verses
   Full of empty words.

3 One may recite a hundred verses full of vain
      descriptions,
   But a single verse bringing peace to
      the listener
   Is worth far more.

4 One may conquer a million men in a single
      battle;
   However, the greatest and best warrior
   Conquers himself.

5,
6 Conquest of one's self is the greatest victory
   of all.
   Neither a god nor a heavenly musician
   Nor a mischievous angel
   Of the highest of the six heavenly abodes—
   The Paranimmita-heaven, where sensual
      pleasures prevail—
   Can deprive the self-vanquished, restrained
      person of victory.

7 The honor paid to the one who has achieved
      self-mastery
   For one single instant
   Is worth more than monthly offerings
   Of a thousand pieces of gold.

8 Honoring the one who has achieved
      self-mastery
   For one single instant
   Is worth more than living in the forest,
   Tending the sacred fire for a hundred years.

9 Making offerings for glory and recognition
   Is not one-quarter as worthy as honoring the
      upright

10 Whoever shows reverence and respect for
      the aged
   Is rewarded fourfold . . .
   With long life, beauty, happiness and strength.

11 Even a single day of a life lived virtuously
  and meditatively,
  Is worth more than a hundred years lived
  wantonly and
  Without discipline.

12 A single day's life of a wise and contemplative
  man
  Is worth more than a hundred years lived
  wantonly and
  Without discipline.

13 A single day's life of one who puts out great
  effort
  Is better than a life of a hundred years
  Lived in idleness and sluggishness.

14 A single day's life lived by a man who grasps
  The impermanence of all conditioned things
  Is worth more than a hundred years lived
  In blindness and ignorance.

15 A single day's life of one who sees the
  deathless state
  Is worth more than a hundred years
  Lived without perceiving it

16 A single day's life of one who sees the truth
  Is worth more than a hundred years
  Of not seeing the truth.

9

Evil

1 Do not lose a moment of doing good.
Protect your mind from evil.
Whoever neglects doing good
Is inviting addiction to evil.

2 If a man has mistakenly committed an evil deed,
Let him not repeat it.
Let him not be addicted to evil,
For it is the amassing of evil that brings misery.

3 On the other hand, if a man does good,
Let him do it repeatedly.
Let him put his heart into it,
For the accumulation of good brings blessings.

4 Even an evildoer feels happy
Before his negative actions reach fruition.
However when the evil ripens
He will have a bountiful harvest of evil results.

5 A good man sees what is unwholesome
Before his good deeds reach fruition.
However, when the good ripens
He will have a bountiful harvest of good results.

6 Don't underestimate evil, saying,
"It can't happen to me."
As a pot slowly fills up with water, drop
    by drop,
So does the fool, little by little,
Become full of evil.

7 Don't underestimate good,
Saying, "It can't happen to me."
Water falling, drop by drop, will fill even a
    large pot.
Likewise, the wise man, accumulating good,
    little by little,
Becomes goodness itself.

8 A merchant with treasures and a small caravan
Avoids a dangerous road.
A man, loving life, shuns poison,
As one should shun all evil.

9 If a man has a hand free of wounds,
He can take poison in his hand.
The poison cannot penetrate the hand that is
    free of wounds.
Likewise, a man is not guilty
When he acts with no evil intention.

10   If someone harms an innocent person,
      One pure and free of guilt,
      Evil results will fall upon the doer
      Like fine dust thrown into the wind.

11   Some are reborn in a mother's womb.
      The evildoers are bound to miserable states.
      The doers of good are reborn to happy states.
      Those free of any stain go on to perfect peace.

12   There is no place in the world—
      Neither the sky, the sea, nor in mountain
          crevices—
      Where an evildoer can hide,
      Safe from the consequences of his action.

13   There is no place in the world—
      Neither in the sky, the sea, nor in mountain
          crevices—
      Where one can escape the inevitability of
          death.

10

The Rod

1   Everybody fears being struck by a rod.
Everybody fears death.
  Therefore, knowing this, feeling for others as
    for yourself,
Do not kill others or cause others to kill.

2   Everybody fears being struck by a rod,
Life being dear to all.
  Therefore, knowing this, feeling for others as
    for yourself,
Do not kill others or cause others to kill.

3   If one, pursuing happiness, strikes
Living beings who also strive to live happily
With a rod or other instrument,
He will reap an unwholesome harvest.

4   If one pursues his own happiness,
While causing no harm to other living beings
Who also strive to live happily,
He will reap a wholesome harvest.

5   Avoid harsh speech.
     Angry words backfire upon the speaker.

6   By making yourself as still as a cracked cymbal,
     Not retaliating, you achieve nirvana.

7   As a cowherd leads the cattle to pasture,
     So do old age and death
     Inevitably come to all beings.

8,   Brethren, the ignorant may not be aware of
9   doing evil.
     Eventually they are consumed
       by their evil deeds as by fire.
     He who inflicts pain on the innocent
     Comes to one of ten calamities.

10,   Pain, loss, injury, illness, insanity,
11,   Danger from rulers,
12
     Frightening accusations, loss of loved ones,
     Loss of wealth—
     One of these will he experience—
     Or fire will destroy his house.
     After the destruction of his body,
     The same foolish man
     Will go to an unhappy state.

13   Though he does penance through nakedness,
     With tangled hair, covering his body with mud,
     Fasting, rubbing himself with ash,
     And crouching in a posture of humility,

None of these rites can purify a man
Who has not freed himself of doubt.

14 Regardless of attire or adornment,
The guiltless one, calm, self-restrained,
Chaste, and resolute,
Refraining totally from hurting living beings,
Is the brahman, the recluse, the monk.

15 It is the rare being who is restrained by
    self-direction,
Who does not invite reproof,
As a good horse does not invite the whip.

16 Be like a good horse, touched gently by the
    whip—
The horse moves forward with full power and
    energy.
Have an abundance of confidence,
Good conduct, effort, concentration.
Be aware and attentive,
Put aside this great mass of suffering.

17 Those who would irrigate the land
Bring the water wherever they choose.
Arrowsmiths fashion arrows.
Carpenters shape wood.
The virtuous mold themselves.

11

Old Age

1 Can there be joy and laughter when the world
   is ablaze?
   Should you not seek the light before darkness
   falls?

2 Look at the body adorned,
   A mass of wounds, a heap of bones,
   Impermanent, unstable,
   Though most of us fail to recognize this.

3 The body wears out,
   A nest of disease,
   Fragile, disintegrating,
   Ending in death.

4 What delight is there in seeing the bleached
   bones,
   Dried and scattered in the autumn sun?

5 A citadel is this structure of bones, blood,
       and flesh,
   Destined for old age, death, conceit, and malice.

6 The royal chariots surely come to decay
   Just as the body, too, comes to decay.
   But the shining truth and living kindness
       live on,
   So speak the virtuous to the virtuous.

7 The unwise person grows large in body.
   Though he becomes large physically,
   His mind remains small.

8, How many lives, how many rounds of rebirth
9   Have I experienced
    Without finding the builder of this house?
    Now I see you, O builder,
    All of your rafters are broken, your ridgepole is
        shattered.
    Never again need you build a house for me.
    My mind has gone beyond the transitory, the
        conditioned,
    And has achieved the extinction of craving.

10 Those who do not find their way to
       a higher life,
   Or who fail to earn wealth during their youth,
   Look back with regret in their old age,
   Like large old wading birds beside a
       dried pond.

11 Having attained neither the higher life of
   the seeker,
  Nor having acquired wealth and power in their
   youth,
  They lie like spent arrows that have missed
   their mark,
  Bewailing their misspent past.

12

Self

1   If a man holds himself in high esteem,
    Let him be vigilant,
    A careful observer,
    Day and night.

2   First one must establish one's own high moral
        principles,
    Then preach to others.
    That is the path of the wise person.

3   Let one mold himself
    In accordance with the precepts he teaches.
    There can be no gap in credibility,
    And no disgrace.

4   Only the self shelters the self.
    What other refuge could there be outside
        the self?

5 As a diamond bores a softer gem,
    So does the evil committed by a fool crush
      the doer.

6 As a strangling vine chokes a tree,
    So does a person's unwholesome action
      destroy him,
    To the delight of his enemy.

7 Unwholesome action, hurting self, comes easily.
    Wholesome action, healing self, takes effort.

8 A foolish man clings to wrong views,
    Mocks the teachings of the righteous.
    Such a person reaps what he sows,
    Inviting ruin and destruction
    Like the fruit-bearing bamboo tree.

9 By oneself is evil done, by oneself is one made
      impure.
    By oneself is evil undone, by oneself is one
      made pure.
    Each one is responsible for purity and impurity.
    No one can cleanse another.

10 One should heal oneself before attempting
      to heal another.
    Learn first before teaching another.
    Let each one embrace his own truth
    And devote himself to its fulfillment.

13

The World

1 Do not follow low practices.
   Do not live carelessly.
   Do not hold wrong views.
   Do not prolong the suffering of the world.

2 Lift yourself up. Be attentive.
   Act virtuously.
   One who does good deeds lives happily,
   Both in this life and the life to come.

3 Act righteously.
   Refuse to do otherwise.
   One who follows this path lives happily,
   Both in this life and the life to come.

4 Perceive the world as a bubble.
   Perceive the world as a mirage.
   If you see the world in this way,
   You render the Lord of Death powerless.

5 Look at the body as a royal chariot
   To which the ignorant cling,
   While the wise let go.

6 Whoever moves from carelessness to
        mindfulness,
   From ignorance to wisdom,
   Lights up the world
   Like the moon emerging from a cloud.

7 Whoever overcomes his unwholesome
        behavior
   And replaces it with wholesome action
   Illuminates the world
   Like the moon emerging from a cloud.

8 There is blindness all around,
   Very few can see.
   Many are like birds trapped in a net,
   While few escape and achieve liberation.

9 Swans fly in the sky.
   Those possessed of psychic powers
   Glide through the air.
   The wise, conquering self, proceed to nirvana.

10 A man who violates even one spiritual law,
   Who is dishonest, denying the truth
   About life, death, and eternity,
   Will be incapable of restraining himself from
        evil.

11   Those closed off from generosity
     Do not enter the realm of gods,
     And will find neither fulfillment
     Nor the happiness and the peace of the wise
        and generous.

12   Better than the loftiest goal
     Of lording over the world,
     Or traversing the heavens,
     Is placing oneself on the path.

14

The Buddha

1 The Buddha's conquest is beyond all
    conquests.
The Buddha's development cannot be
    measured
In worldly terms—
Whose range of vision is infinite,
Who has no feet of clay—
On what feet can anyone deign to lead the
    Buddha?

2 The Buddha is one who has crushed the bonds
    of desire,
The lures that lead one astray.
On what feet would you have the Buddha
    move,
For he has no feet.

3 Even gods cherish the vigilant Buddhas,
Meditative, wise, peaceful,
And free of passion.

4   It is difficult to be born human.
    It is difficult to conduct life as a human being.
    Rare is the opportunity to hear the Dhamma.
    Even more rare is the appearance of a Buddha.

5   To shun all evil.
    To do good.
    To purify one's heart.
    This is the teaching of the Buddhas.

6   Patience that is enduring
    Is the best discipline.
    Nirvana, say the Buddhas, is the highest goal.
    Whoever hurts another is not a monk.
    Whoever insults another is not a renunciate.

7   Right speech, harmlessness,
    Restraint in speaking ill of others,
    Moderation in food, at peace in remoteness
       and solitude,
    Devotion to higher meditation.
    This is the teaching of the Buddhas.

8, A shower of gold pieces cannot satisfy craving.
9   Sensual pleasures bring little sweetness,
    Cause much suffering.
    The disciple of the Buddha finds joy
    In the extinction of desire.

10 There is no place to hide,
    Neither mountains, forest, trees, nor shrines.

11   Surely there is no safe refuge, no great refuge.
      Wherever he goes, man takes his passions
         with him.

12,   However, if one turns to the Buddha,
13,   The Dhamma, the Sangha,
14   Realizes the four great truths,
      Knows the roots and cause of dukkha—
      Which is suffering—
      And knows its cessation by pursuing the
         eightfold path,
      One finds refuge and frees himself from all
         suffering.

15   A supreme being is hard to find.
      He is not born in many places.
      The family of such a wise one knows
         happiness.

16   Blessed is the appearance of the Buddhas.
      Blessed is the teaching of the Dhamma.
      Blessed is the unity of the Order.
      Blessed is the disciplined life of its followers.

17,   No one can measure the merit one acquires
18   By honoring the Buddhas,
      As one who has gone beyond the ocean of
         sorrow and grief,
      And has arrived at the shore of inner peace
      And absolute serenity.

15

Happiness

1 Truly we dwell in happiness.
 Others hate, but we do not.
 Surrounded by those who hate
 We live free from hatred.

2 Truly we dwell in happiness.
 Others are sick, but we are not.
 Surrounded by sick people
 We live free from sickness.

3 Truly we dwell in happiness,
 Free from struggles, while others struggle.
 Surrounded by struggling people
 We live free from conflict.

4 Truly we dwell in happiness,
 Having no obstacles at all.
 We shall feed on joy
 Like radiant gods.

5 Victory produces hostility,
For the defeated ones live in grief.
Releasing both victory and defeat,
The tranquil minds dwell in happiness.

6 There is no fire like lust, no evil like hatred.
There are no disasters equal to those we create
In our existences.
There is no happiness greater than the peace
of nirvana.

7 Hunger is the most severe bodily disease.
Conditioned things are the worst calamity.
When we see this clearly,
We achieve nirvana, the ultimate bliss.

8 Health is the highest prize.
A monk is to be satisfied even with the little
he obtains.
A loyal friend is the best relative.
Nirvana is the supreme bliss.

9 Having tasted the sweetness of solitude and
tranquility,
One becomes free of sorrow and sin,
While fully savoring the nectar
Of the joy of spiritual excellence.

10 To choose the company of holy ones,
To live with them, is a holy state.
By not seeking out unwholesome company,
One maintains a state of happiness.

11 Therefore, like the moon
    Following its ordained course,
    Let each one follow a good person,
    Wise, steadfast, loyal, and holy.

16

The Pleasant

1   When anyone mistakenly pursues only what
        is pleasant,
    Avoiding the true path,
    Forgetting their true purpose, attached to the
        senses,
    When anyone sees another on the true path,
    They will experience their loss and be full of
        reproach.

2   Avoid attachment to both what is pleasant
    And what is unpleasant.
    Losing the pleasant causes grief.
    Dwelling on the unpleasant also causes grief.

3   Do not cling to the pleasant.
    Let it pass,
    So that the separation will not diminish you.

4   Clinging to what is dear brings sorrow.
    Clinging to what is dear brings fear.

To one who is entirely free from endearment
There is no sorrow or fear.

5 Sorrow springs from affection.
Fear springs from affection.
To loosen those bonds
Is to be free from sorrow and fear.

6 Sorrow springs from indulgence in sensual
  pleasures.
Fear springs from indulgence in sensual
  pleasures.
Whoever is free from such indulgence
Knows neither sorrow nor fear.

7 Sorrow springs from preoccupation with
  lustful pleasures.
Fear springs from preoccupation with lustful
  pleasures.
Whoever is free from such preoccupation
Knows neither sorrow nor fear.

8 Sorrow springs from craving.
Fear springs from craving.
Whoever is free from craving
Knows neither sorrow nor fear.

9 People cherish the person committed to right
  action
And rich in understanding.
That person, knowing the truth,
Walks steadfastly on the path.

10   The person who reaches the sacred, the
        inexpressible,
     Who has permeated his mind with it,
     Who is in control of his senses,
     Is one bound upstream.

11   Friends and relatives welcome with joy a
        loved one,
     Returning from abroad after a long absence.
     In exactly the same way will the fruits of right
        action
     Welcome the doer as he travels from one life
        to the next.

17

Anger

1 Shun anger, let go of pride,
   Break out of every shackle.
   Whoever is not tied to possessions,
   Clinging neither to body nor mind,
   Is never in bondage.

2 Whoever controls his anger
   Is like a true charioteer,
   In command of the rolling chariot
   And not just holding on the reins.

3 Where there is anger, apply loving kindness.
   Where there is evil, offer good.
   Where there is stinginess, be generous.
   Where there are lies, be truthful.

4 Speak the truth, control anger.
   Share even from your meager store.
   These three steps lead to the presence of the
   "Shining Ones."

5 The wise ones who do no harm,
  Ever restrained in body, word, and mind,
  Come to the place of peace
  Where they will sorrow no more.

6 The vigilant, who prepare themselves
  Day and night,
  Will free themselves of unwholesome action
  And achieve nirvana.

7 This, O Atula,* has been going on through
      the ages.
  They criticize the silent ones.
  They criticize the talkative ones.
  They criticize the moderate ones.
  There is no one in the world who escapes
      criticism.

8 There never was and never will be,
  Nor is there now,
  The wholly criticized
  Or the wholly approved.

9, Whom the discriminating praise
10 As behaving impeccably in life,
  Displaying wisdom, insight, and discipline,

---

*Atula: Atula was a lay devotee who lived at the time of the
Buddha. When he told the Buddha about the flaws in other
people, the Buddha admonished him of the value of
forbearance.

Will be praised even by Brahma
And treasured like a coin of pure gold.

11 Avoid rash action.
Be restrained in speech and action.
Exercise right action.

12 Avoid rash speech.
Be restrained in speech.
Exercise right speech.

13 Avoid mental agitation.
Be restrained in mind.
Think good thoughts.

14 Those who practice restraint
In body, word, and mind
Are surely in control of themselves.

18

Blemishes

1 You are now like a withered leaf,
  Very close to the approaching messenger of
    death.
  Although at the point of departure,
  You have not prepared yourself for the journey.

2 Prepare a refuge for yourself,
  Work hard, use good judgment.
  Free of flaws and passions,
  You shall enter the highest realms.

3 You have reached the end of your time.
  You stand face to face with death.
  You have no place to rest upon the road,
  Nor any preparation for the journey.

4 Prepare a refuge for yourself.
  Work hard, use good judgment.
  Free of flaws and passions,
  You need never return to the cycles of birth
    and death.

5 The wise man, carefully, moment by moment,
One by one,
Eliminates the stains of his mind,
As a silversmith separates the dross from the
silver.

6 Just as rust produced by iron
Corrodes the iron,
So is the violator of moral law
Destroyed by his own wrong action.

7 Unlived scriptures are not heard.
Neglected houses fall apart.
Uncared-for beauty withers.
Uncultivated, the mind goes to seed.

8 A woman behaving badly loses her femininity.
A giver sharing grudgingly loses his generosity.
Deeds done from bad motives remain
everlastingly tainted.

9 But there is nothing more tainted than
ignorance.
Eliminate ignorance, O disciples,
And purity follows.

10 Life is easy to live for a shameless man,
Aggressive, arrogant,
Intrusive, and corrupt.

11   Life is not easy to live for a modest man
    With high values, free from attachment,
    Humble, of right livelihood,
    And clear vision.

12,   Whoever in the world takes life,
13   Tells lies, steals, commits adultery,
    Is addicted to drinking intoxicating liquors,
    Is digging up his very roots, even when alive.

14   Be aware, everyone, that those flawed in their
       nature
    Have no control of themselves.
    Do not let greed and anger cause you suffering
    By holding you in their grasp.

15   Men give for different reasons,
    Such as devotion or appreciation.
    Whoever finds fault with the food or drink given
       by others
    Will have no peace, day or night.

16   However, whoever gives up this habit of
       finding fault
    With others' offerings
    Will know peace, day and night.

17   There is no fire like lust,
    No vise like hatred,
    No trap like delusion,
    And no galloping river like craving.

18 It is easy to see the flaws of others,
Hard to see our own.
Exposing the flaws of others,
As one winnows the chaff,
Yet hiding our own faults,
We are cunning gamblers, concealing the dice.

19 Far from removal and constantly growing
Are the blemishes of the man who clearly sees
And points out the faults of others,
But is ever resistant to corrections in himself.

20 There is no path through the air.
There is no real monk outside the eightfold
    path.
People love their obstacles.
Only the enlightened ones transcend them.

21 There is no path through the air.
There is no real monk outside the eightfold
    path.
There are no compounded things that are
    unchanging.
Only the enlightened ones, the Buddhas, are
    unconditioned.

19

The Righteous

1 He is not righteous
   Who judges a situation impulsively.
   But whoever distinguishes between right and
      wrong,
   That one is righteous.

2 Whoever leads others
   Evenhandedly, but not by force,
   Is a guardian of justice
   And is called righteous.

3 A man is not considered wise
   Because he talks a lot.
   But he is secure and called wise
   Who is free of hate and does no harm.

4 A man cannot be regarded well-versed in the
      Dhamma
   By his rhetoric.
   However, even with little learning,

A man who does not neglect the practice of
   virtue
May be considered well-versed in the Dhamma.

5 Gray hair does not make a man an elder.
   He is but ripe in age,
   And may simply be called a foolish, doddering
      old man.

6 To be considered truly an elder
   A man must practice truthfulness,
   Righteousness, harmlessness,
   Restraint, and self-control,
   Be free of stain and rich in wisdom.

7 Neither good looks
   Nor a glib tongue
   Make a man attractive,
   If he is envious, stingy, and dishonest.

8 However, once he has cut down
   And rooted out these traits,
   And found wisdom,
   Then can he be called attractive.

9 A shaven head does not make a man a monk,
   If he is still undisciplined and dishonest.
   How can he be called a monk,
   If he is filled with desire and greed?

10 A man may be called a monk
   If he is cleansed of evil, large or small,
   Free from unwholesome tendencies.

11 Living simply on alms does not make a man
        holy,
    If he also behaves badly.

12 He who lives the higher life,
    Full of understanding of the world
    But free of its good or evil,
    That one can be called a holy man.

13 A man cannot be called wise simply because
        he is silent.
    Whoever is aware, conscious of what is,
    Choosing wisely,
    That one can be called a sage.

14 Having discerned both worlds,
    Both the inner and outer life,
    And having chosen good over evil,
    A man may be called a sage.

15 If one harms living beings,
    He cannot be considered noble.
    Only by exercising harmlessness toward living
        beings
    Can one be called noble.

16, Neither learning nor embracing solemn vows,
17 Nor achieving a great state of concentration,
    Nor living alone will assure nirvana.
    Nirvana is only achieved by right action.

20

The Way

1 The eightfold path is the best of ways.
  The four noble truths are the best of truths.
  Freedom from desire is the best of states.
  Whoever is clear-eyed and wise is the best of
      men.

2 There is the one and only way.
  There is no other leading to perfect insight.
  Follow this path, leaving Mara, the tempter,
      powerless.

3 Following this path, you shall put an end to
      suffering.
  I have shown you the way
  That leads to freedom
  From the arrows of passion.

4 You, yourselves, must walk the path.
  Buddhas only show the way.

Those who are meditative, who have gotten
   on the path,
Will be free from the bonds of Mara.

5   Everything changes. Nothing stays the same.
Having gained this awareness, one is freed
   from suffering.
This is the way of purification.

6   All conditioned things are subject to change.
Having fully learned this insight,
One is freed from suffering.
This is the way of purification.

7   Everything is insubstantial.
Having fully recognized this,
One is freed from suffering.
This is the way of purification.

8   The lazy man, weak in mental discipline,
Indolent, prone to sloth,
Unproductive, and though young and strong,
Failing to move at the right time,
Never finds the road to wisdom.

9   Curb your speech.
Restrain your mind.
Commit no evil deed.
These three patterns bring you to a place of
   wisdom.

10 Wisdom is born from meditation.
Not to meditate is loss.
Know the difference between gain and loss.
Make the choice to walk where wisdom grows.

11 Cut down the whole jungle of craving,
Not just an isolated tree in the forest.
The jungle of craving harbors danger.
Clear the trees of craving, both strong and
    weak,
And find freedom.

12 As long as there is the least clinging to
    lustful thoughts,
Man will remain in mental bondage,
Like a nursing calf attached to its mother.

13 Cut off the ego with your own hand,
As you would an autumn lily.
Follow the peaceful path leading to nirvana,
Guided by the one who has walked the path.

14 "I shall live here in the rains,
There in winter,
Elsewhere in summer," muses the fool,
Not aware of the nearness of death.

15 Death carries the unaware man away,
While he is still busily acquiring children and
    animals,

Much as a rampaging flood engulfs a sleeping
village.

16, When death comes,
17 Neither children, father, or other loved ones
Can offer refuge.
Aware of this,
The wise behave well.
Don't postpone right action,
But clear the path to nirvana.

21

Miscellany

1 A wise man gives up lesser comforts
  For a higher purpose.

2 How foolish to seek comfort
  Through someone else's pain.
  There is no escape from the trap of animosity.

3 The indolent and negligent
  Accrue unwholesome mind states
  By doing what should not be done,
  And failing to do what should be done.

4 Unwholesome mind states disappear
  Among those who are mindful of the nature of
    the body,
  Who stop doing what is right not to be done,
  And fulfill what needs to be done.

5 He has killed his mother (craving),
  His father (pride),

And two kings (eternalistic and nihilistic
   views).
He has subdued the tyranny of his sense organs
And their objects,
And he emerges the noble one, unscathed.

6 He has vanquished the hindrances—
   Lust, anger, sloth, and torpor,
   Skepticism and distraction of mind—
   And he emerges the noble one, unscathed.

7 The disciples of Gautama are truly awake,
   Day and night,
   Focusing on the Buddha.

8 The disciples of Gautama are truly awake,
   Day and night,
   Thinking of the Dhamma.

9 The disciples of Gautama are truly awake,
   Day and night,
   Meditating on the specific virtues
   Of the members of the Sangha.

10 The disciples of Gautama are truly awake,
   Day and night,
   Concentrating on the nature of their physical
     bodies.

11 The disciples of Gautama are truly awake,
   Day and night,
   Joyfully practicing nonviolence.

12 The disciples of Gautama are truly awake,
    Day and night,
    Setting their minds joyfully on meditation.

13 It is hard to renounce the world.
    It is hard and troublesome to live the
        household life.
    It is painful to live with those
    Who are in a different way of life.
    In these ways is the wayfarer beset with
        troubles.
    End your suffering.
    Cease being a wayfarer.

14 A person devoted to his faith,
    Disciplined, illustrious, and prosperous,
    Is honored
    Wherever he chooses to live.

15 Good people are visible from the distance,
    Like the Himalaya mountains.
    Bad people become invisible,
    Like an arrow shot in the night.

16 Sit alone,
    Sleep alone,
    Walk alone,
    Enthusiastically.
    Shape yourself alone.
    Enjoy the seclusion of life in the forest.

22

State of Woe

1 The liar is headed for sorrow.
  The man who denies what he has done
  Is headed for sorrow.
  Both doers of evil deeds
  Are in the same state after death.

2 Many, though wearing the saffron robe,
  Are mean and undisciplined.
  Being that way,
  They are headed for sorrow.

3 It is better for an immoral person
  To swallow a red-hot ball,
  Fully ablaze,
  Than to eat the food provided by pious people.

4, Four misfortunes befall the careless person
5 Who pursues others' wives—
  Unwholesome states, sleeplessness,
      condemnation,

And rebirth into a sorrowful state.
The faithless man knows fleeting pleasure
With the faithless woman.
Severe consequences follow.
Do not court another's wife.

6 Just as a blade of Kusa grass handled improperly,
    cuts the hand,
So does the life of a recluse handled improperly,
    bring him to a sorrowful state.

7 A deed done carelessly,
A corrupt act,
The higher life led without integrity,
All yield poor results.

8 If anything is undertaken,
Do it impeccably.
Poorly led monastic life
Stirs up the dust of passions more widely.

9 Better to avoid doing evil,
And not suffer the torment that follows.
Better to do what is right,
And not suffer the regret.

10 Just as a border town is protected, within and
    without,
So let one guard oneself,
And not let the opportunity pass.
To neglect that opportunity is to invite
    suffering.

11 Some are ashamed of what is not shameful,
    And shameless about what is shameful.
    Following such false views,
    They go to a sorrowful state.

12 Some are fearful where there is nothing to fear,
    And are fearless where there is much to fear.
    Holding such false views,
    They go to a sorrowful state.

13 Some see what is right as wrong
    And what is wrong as right.
    Holding such false views,
    They go to a sorrowful state.

14 Those who see wrong as wrong
    And right as right
    Hold right views,
    And go to a joyful state.

23

The Elephant

1 I shall bear harsh words,
As the elephant in battle endures arrows,
For I know that most people behave poorly.

2 It is the tamed elephant that men lead into a
crowd.
A king mounts only a tamed elephant.
The man who has tamed himself,
And patiently bears harsh words,
Is also the best among men.

3 The tamed mules are good.
The well-bred horses of Sindh are good.
The mighty elephants are good.
Best of all is the man who has tamed himself.

4 One does not ride tamed animals to nirvana.
Only the tamed person goes there,
On his well-tamed self.

5 The elephant, Dhanapalaka, in rut,
His temples steaming, restless, bound,
Does not eat his food at all,
Longing for the elephant forest.

6 When one is sluggish, gluttonous,
Rolling about like a large pig stuffed with swill,
One is reborn a simpleton, again and again,
Continuously suffering.

7 This mind once wandered restlessly, wherever
it chose,
But now I hold it in check,
As a trainer restrains the rutting elephant
With the hook.

8 Be vigilant.
Protect your mind.
Free yourself from the difficulty of an elephant
Sunk in quagmire.

9 If a man finds a companion
Prudent, wise, upright, and righteous,
Let him go with him, happy but vigilant,
Overcoming all danger.

10 If a man cannot find a companion
Prudent, wise, upright, and righteous,
Let him walk alone,
Like the king leaving the conquered land,
Or an elephant roaming by himself in the
forest.

11   It is better to live alone,
     Than to have a fool for a companion.
     Living alone, avoid evil ways of life.
     Be harmless, at ease, like the elephant in the
       forest.

12   It is pleasant to have companions when you
       need them.
     It is pleasant to be satisfied with whatever
       comes your way.
     It is pleasant to know virtue at the moment of
       death.
     It is pleasant to be beyond all suffering.

13   It is pleasant to be a loving child toward your
       mother.
     It is pleasant to be a loving child toward your
       father.
     It is pleasant to show proper respect to the
       recluse.
     It is pleasant to behave respectfully to holy
       beings.

14   It is pleasant to reach old age as a moral being.
     It is pleasant to enjoy self-esteem and
       confidence.
     It is pleasant to achieve insight.
     It is pleasant to abstain from evil.

24

Craving

1 Unchecked craving strangles the careless man,
   Like a creeper growing in the jungle.
   He leaps from lifetime to lifetime,
   Like a monkey seeking fruit.

2 This craving, this clinging,
   Overpowers the man caught in it,
   And his sorrows multiply,
   Like prairie grass fed by rain.

3 Although it is hard to gain this freedom,
   Sorrow leaves the man who overcomes this
       toxic craving,
   This clinging to the world,
   Just as drops of water fall from a lotus leaf.

4 Therefore, I admonish you.
   You have my blessings.
   Eradicate craving at the root, as you would
       weeds.

Find the sweet root.
Do not succumb to temptation over and over
  again.

5 The tree may be cut down but the roots remain,
Uninjured and strong,
And it springs up again.
Likewise, suffering returns, again and again,
If the dormant craving is not completely
  eradicated.

6 A man will be swept along
By the thirty-six streams of sensual pleasure,
Borne on the strong currents
Of his craving toward tempting objects.

7 The streams of craving flow everywhere.
The creeper of craving grows wild,
Through the six sense doors.
Being aware of the strangling vine,
Cut it off at the root through insight.

8 Pleasurable sensations arise in living beings.
The feelings are heightened by craving,
And these beings cling to these sensations.
Not letting go,
They are compelled to experience suffering
Over and over again.

9 Human beings, bound by craving,
Rush about aimlessly like trapped rabbits.

Caught up in their desires, they suffer
Over and over again.

10 Human beings, ensnared by craving,
Rush about aimlessly, like trapped rabbits.
Therefore, monk, set aside craving
And find freedom.

11 Come and look at a man who has freed himself
once,
But goes back to his former life of bondage.

12 There are bonds of iron, wood, or grass.
These the wise do not call strong.
Far stronger are the bonds of possessions and
family.

13 Wise men recognize the real attachments
That can drag them down,
Loose, but difficult to untie.
When they master their bonds of craving,
They free themselves from the bondage of the
senses.

14 Those who are lost to lust are trapped,
Like a spider in a web.
The wise ones ford the stream of craving,
Leaving behind all suffering and finding
freedom.

15 Let go of the past.
Let go of the future.

Let go of the present.
Proceed to the opposite shore with a free mind,
Leaving behind all suffering.

16 Craving grows in the man aroused by worldly
       thoughts.
    Tied to his senses, he makes his fetters strong.

17 Freed from fear, aware,
    Worldly thoughts under control,
    Meditating on the impermanence of the body,
    A man achieves liberation.

18 The diligent monk
    Has reached the summit,
    Fearless, free of passion.
    This is the final birth of such a man.

19 Free of craving, he does not cling to worldly
       things.
    He has mastered the meanings within meanings,
    The order of things, the ultimate teaching.
    This mighty being, possessed of perfect insight,
    Need return no more.

20 I have conquered all. I am totally aware
    And have detached myself from all worldly
       things.
    I am free of destructive craving.
    Having attained this state of wisdom by myself,
    Whom should I call my teacher?

21 The gift of truth is the highest gift.
The taste of truth is the sweetest taste.
The joy of truth is the greatest joy.
The extinction of craving is the end of
suffering.

22 Possessions destroy the fool,
But not those who see beyond them.
Through craving for possessions
The fool destroys himself and others as well.

23 Weeds choke the fields.
Lust corrupts humankind.
The gifts bestowed on those free from desire
Bring great rewards.

24 Just as the fields are spoiled by weeds,
So is humankind spoiled by ill will.
There are, therefore,
Great rewards for those free of ill will.

25 Weeds ruin fields.
Ignorance ruins humankind.
Gifts bestowed on those free from ignorance
Bring great rewards.

26 Weeds ruin fields.
Greediness ruins mankind.
Gifts bestowed on those free of greediness
Bring great results.

25

The Bhikkhu

1 It is good to restrain the eye.
It is good to restrain the ear.
It is good to restrain the nose.
It is good to restrain the tongue.

2 It is good to restrain the body.
It is good to restrain the mind.
It is good to restrain thought.
Restraint in all things is good.
The bhikkhu with restraint in all things
Will be free from suffering.

3 He has practiced restraint in all things—
Controlled hands, feet, and speech.
He is meditative and serene,
A true monk.

4 How pleasant is the discourse of the monk,
Spare in his use of words,

Whose speech is restrained,
Who talks wisely,
Who is simple and clear in expressing the
    Dhamma.

5 The monk who abides in the Dhamma,
Who delights in the Dhamma,
Who contemplates the Dhamma,
Will not lose his way.

6 One should not despise his own portion,
Not covet what others have.
A monk who covets what others have
Does not achieve peace of mind.

7 The gods praise the monk
Who is content with his simple lot,
Living by pure means of livelihood.

8 He who is not attached to material possessions,
And does not mourn their loss or decay,
That one is a true bhikkhu.

9 A monk who lives in loving kindness,
Trusting the teachings of the Buddha,
Will attain a state of kindness and equanimity
And find the greatest peace.

10 Empty this boat, O monk,
Free yourself of unwholesome thoughts.

Thus will it sail lightly, with no clinging and
    aversion,
And attain nirvana.

11 Cut off the five fetters: egoism, doubt, anger,
Attachment to rites and ceremonies, and
    sensual indulgence.
Reject the five cravings of rebirth in the
    realm of form,
Or without form—willfulness, conceit, and
    restlessness.
Cultivate the positive five:
Confidence, awareness, effort, concentration,
    and insight.
The monk who has gone beyond the five
    fetters is called
"The one who has crossed the flood."

12 Do not neglect meditation, O monk.
Do not allow your heart to whirl in pleasures
    of the senses.
Do not swallow a flaming iron ball and then,
As you burn, cry out, "Oh, that hurts!"

13 Without reason there is no concentration.
Without concentration there is no reason.
Whoever has both, concentration of mind
    and reasoning power,
Approaches nirvana.

14 A monk who enters a bare cell with serene mind,
   Contemplating on the nature of things,
   Will experience transcendent joy.

15 Whenever he contemplates the rise and fall of
      existence,
   He is filled with the joyful nectar of wisdom.

16, This is the way for the wise bhikkhu to begin.
17 Control the senses.
   Practice equanimity.
   Live by the disciplinary rules.
   Associate with good friends, who are not lazy,
   Who live purely.
   Be courteous and well-mannered.
   And thus, in fullness of joy,
   Put an end to suffering.

18 Just as the jasmine plant sheds its withered
      flowers,
   O monk, shed both lust and hatred.

19 The monk who is peaceful in action, word,
      and thought,
   Who is composed, having discarded the
      world's temptations,
   Can be called "The peaceful one."

20 Admonish yourself strongly.
   Scrutinize yourself deeply.
   Thus, alert and protected by your vigilance,
   You will live in happiness, O monk.

21 Each one is his own refuge.
Each one is his own shelter.
Therefore, each one needs to train himself,
As a trainer does a thoroughbred horse.

22 The monk, full of joy, fulfilled by Buddha's
teaching,
Attains the blissful state of equanimity,
Having let go of the world's complexities.

23 A monk, though still young,
Applying himself devotedly to Buddha's
teaching,
Lights up this work,
Like the moon emerging from a
cloud-filled sky.

26

The Noble One

1 Make headway against the current with your
    energy.
   Scrupulously avoid desire, O noble one.
   Staying alert to the perishability of all the
    elements
   That are temporary,
   You are the knower of the indestructible.

2 Whenever the brahman reaches the perfected
    state of
   Concentration and insight,
   He frees himself from all his chains.

3 I call him noble one who stands neither on
    this shore,
   Nor any shore,
   Freed from all the chains of worry.

4 I call him noble one who is meditative, serene,
   Free of lust,

Having completed what needs to be done,
Stainless, having achieved the highest good.

5 The sun shines by day.
The moon illuminates the night.
The warrior gleams in his armor,
But the Buddha shines in glory, both day
and night.

6 Beyond unwholesome action, one is called a
noble one.
Samana, a recluse, has found peace of mind.
Pabbyita, a holy man, has renounced all
defilement.

7 Never would a noble one attack a noble one.
Nor would a noble one retaliate if attacked.
Whoever attacks a noble one is disgraced.
A noble one who retaliates is dishonored.

8 What hard-won progress
Does the noble one earn
In practicing restraint!
His pains disappear as he practices harmlessness.

9 Whoever keeps under control
His body, his words, his thoughts—
Him do I call a noble one.

10 Even as a brahman shows respect for the
sacrificial fire,
So honored is the one who has mastered
The teachings of Buddha.

11 Neither matted hair, nor so-called high family,
    Nor states of birth make one a noble one.
    By his own actions in the practice of truth
    Does one become a noble one.

12 Of what avail is matted hair?
    What is the purpose of wearing antelope hide?
    When there is madness within,
    One adorns the outside in vain.

13 I call him a noble one who, dressed in tatters,
        lean,
    With veins showing,
    Sits alone in the forest meditating.

14 I do not call a man a noble one merely by
        reason of birth,
    Or if he was born of a noble mother.
    Only if free of all attachments, from worldly
        grasping,
    Then do I call him a noble one.

15 Whoever is not afraid of breaking his chains,
    Whoever has escaped from ties of attachment—
    Him do I call a noble one.

16 I call him a noble one
    Who has cut off the bondage of anger,
    The ties of craving,
    The rope of error,
    Who has lifted the bars of ignorance,
    And perceived the path.

17 Whoever is free of anger,
    Endures abuse, torture, imprisonment with
       equanimity,
    Having infinite patience and endurance,
    Fortified by his courage—
    Him do I call a noble one.

18 I call him a noble one who is free of anger,
    Dutiful, virtuous, pure, and tamed,
    Who bears his last body.

19 Whoever is as detached from pleasures of the
       senses,
    As water dripping form a lotus leaf,
    Or a mustard seed from a needle point—
    Him do I call a noble one.

20 Whoever experiences the end of his own
       suffering,
    Even while here,
    Who has let go of his burdens, who is unbound—
    Him do I call a noble one.

21 Whoever is rich in insight and wisdom,
    Discerning both the right and wrong paths,
    Having attained the highest good—
    Him do I call a noble one.

22 Whoever detaches himself,
    Both from the householders and the homeless,
    Having simple needs, no house to stay in—
    Him do I call a noble one.

23 Whoever withholds the rod from creatures
Both weak and strong,
Abstaining from killing or causing killing—
Him do I call a noble one.

24 Whoever is friendly among the hostile,
Serene among the agitated,
Detached among the clinging—
Him do I call a noble one.

25 Whoever has freed himself from lust,
Anger, pride, and dishonesty,
As a mustard seed drops from a needle point—
Him do I call a noble one.

26 Whoever speaks gently, honestly,
Imparting knowledge,
Offending no one—
Him do I call a noble one.

27 Whoever accepts nothing, long or short,
Small or large, expensive or cheap,
Unless it is freely given to him—
Him do I call a noble one.

28 Whoever has no craving,
Either for this or another world,
Who is detached and unbound—
Him do I call a noble one.

29 Whoever has no clinging,
Whoever has freed himself from doubt through
    awareness,

Who has embraced the infinite—
Him do I call a noble one.

30 Whoever has gone beyond
The desire for doing either good or evil,
Is free of sorrow,
Immaculate and pure—
Him do I call a noble one.

31 Whoever is as free of blemish as the spotless
        moon,
Serene and tranquil,
All longing for existence gone—
Him do I call a noble one.

32 Whoever has gone beyond his quagmire of
        rebirths,
Passed over this hard road of passion and
        delusion
And reached the other shore,
Who is meditative, secure, free from doubt,
And completely emancipated—
Him do I call a noble one.

33 Whoever has abandoned sensual pleasure,
Who moves about free from the bonds of
        household life,
Having put an end to craving and rebirth—
Him do I call a noble one.

34 Whoever has rooted out desire,
Who moves freely from all household bonds,

Who has put an end to longing and rebirth—
Him do I call a noble one.

35 Whoever is free from all bonds,
Having cast off earthly ties,
Having transcended heavenly ties—
Him do I call a noble one.

36 Whoever has cast off delight and aversion,
Having removed the ground for rebirth,
A man of great strength and courage,
Victor of all levels of existence—
Him do I call a noble one.

37 Whoever understands completely
The passing away and rebirth of beings,
Who remains detached and acts nobly—
Him do I call a noble one.

38 The one whose after-death destiny is
Unknown to gods, guardian spirits, or men,
Who is completely pure, the holy one—
Him do I call a noble one.

39 Whoever is beyond clinging,
For past, present, or future,
Who possesses nothing,
Is released from the world.

40 He is a seer,
Strong, resolute, heroic,
Beyond conflict, cleansed, enlightened.
Him do I call a noble one.

41 Whoever knows all his past lives,
    Sees both the happy and unhappy realms,
    Is free from rebirth,
    Has achieved perfect insight,
    And has attained the summit of the
        higher life,
    Him do I call a noble one.

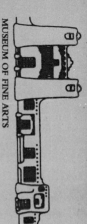

MUSEUM OF FINE ARTS

PALACE OF THE GOVERNORS

MUSEUM OF NEW MEXICO

Adult Single Visit 4/01/97 $5.00

MUSEUM OF INTERNATIONAL FOLK ART

FOLK ART RRS
MUSEUM OF INDIAN ARTS AND CULTURE

00120850

The Museum of New Mexico State Monuments introduce visitors to the legends of the Southwest through interpretive exhibits and historic sites.

1. Fort Selden
2. Fort Sumner
3. Jemez
4. Lincoln
5. Coronado

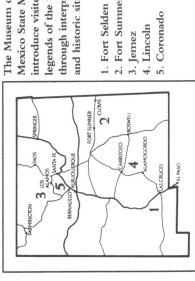

MUSEUM OF FINE ARTS

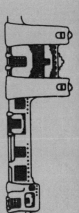

PALACE OF THE GOVERNORS

MUSEUM OF NEW MEXICO

Adult Single Visit   4/01/97 $5.00

MUSEUM OF INTERNATIONAL FOLK ART

FOLK ART   RRS
MUSEUM OF INDIAN ARTS AND CULTURE

00120849

The Museum of New
Mexico State Monuments
introduce visitors to the
legends of the Southwest
through interpretive exhibits
and historic sites.

1. Fort Selden
2. Fort Sumner
3. Jemez
4. Lincoln
5. Coronado

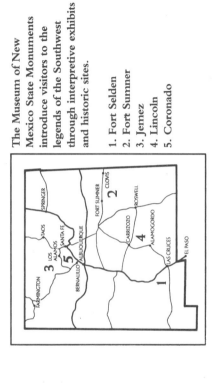

Parallax Press publishes books and tapes on Buddhism
for contemporary readers. Please write for a copy of
our catalog.

Parallax Press
P.O. Box 7355
Berkeley, CA 94707
USA